...er at the christening of Rudolf Hess's son Wolf-Rüdiger in 1938.
...erl/Süddeutscher Verlag-Bilderdienst)

My Father's
Keeper

Hit
(Sc

My Father's Keeper

The Children
of the Nazi Leaders –
An Intimate History of
Damage and Denial

STEPHAN and NORBERT
LEBERT

Translated by Julian Evans

LITTLE, BROWN AND COMPANY

A *Little, Brown* Book

First published in Germany by Karl Blessing Verlag in 2000
as *Denn Du trägst meinen Namen*
First published in Great Britain by
Little, Brown and Company in 2001

A CIP catalogue record for this book is available from
the British Library.

ISBN 0 316 85811 0

Typeset in Sabon by M Rules

Printed and bound in Great Britain by
Clays Ltd, St Ives plc

Little, Brown and Company (UK)
Brettenham House
Lancaster Place
London WC2E 7EN

www.littlebrown.co.uk

Contents

Prologue

IN 1995, THE death of an old woman is recorded. The notice in the Deaths column includes the phrase: 'Where Fate begins, the gods end.' You could say that this particular woman had more than one fate. One lay in the fact that for more than forty years she was able to see her husband only on visits to a Kafkaesque prison. For long years he was the sole inmate of this fortress – until the visits ceased, the day he lay dead in his cell. For seven years the woman lived on as a widow, till she also died. Her notice in the Deaths column declared: 'In courage her life ended.'

The preacher at a funeral should have some connection with the life of the deceased. The woman's son telephoned a former minister, a retired religious teacher, and asked him whether he would speak at the funeral service. He added a condition: the man of God should accept only if he could promise that his oration would not come across as too Christian and would, above all, not contain a single bad word about Adolf Hitler.

On the face of it, this is a funeral service like many others. People in black, with solemn, set faces. The mourners each saying a few words. But there is something unusual. The preacher's name is Martin Bormann – junior, the son of the Nazi hangman Martin Bormann. The dead woman's name is Ilse Hess.

Born Ilse Pröhl at the beginning of the twentieth century, at a young age she got to know a skinny boy, Rudolf by name, a boy with the distinguishing characteristic of black circles around his eyes: many attested even then to a brooding, melancholy presence. When Ilse married him in 1931, she could nevertheless hardly have suspected that her husband would turn out to be one of the guiltiest of the Nazi war criminals, a man who even as a lonely, ailing prisoner would make world politics watch and wait with bated breath for decades.

It is important to understand how, living together from day to day, Hitler's inner circle of National Socialists had a sectarian character. Living communally in the Obersalzberg, whenever there was something to celebrate they celebrated together, demonstrating the unfailing strength of their thousand-year friendship. As a consequence of this way of life Martin Bormann junior, the terrible Bormann's son, came to have two very special godparents: on one side Adolf Hitler, on the other Ilse Hess. Thus the question before Frau Hess's funeral was also whether Martin Bormann would speak about his godmother without saying a bad word about his godfather.

Martin Bormann junior, a man who has often lectured in schools on the subject of 'Fascism: Never Again' but